What people are saying about 10 Tips for *Liking* the Bible (Because Believing It's True Is Not Enough)

10 Tips for Liking the Bible delivers on what the title promises. Keith's tips are immediately practical and accessible, whether you have walked with Jesus for thirty years or thirty minutes. If you are a pastor – to adults or students – keep several on hand and start giving them away. Do you want your congregation and your students to grow in their hunger and love for the Word? If so, this is the next book they need to read!

Gary Thomas
Bestselling Author and Speaker, Writer in Residence
2nd Baptist Church (Houston, TX)

I've been in education, either as a teacher or as an administrator, for twenty-one years. Never have I come across such a comprehensive, practical book as 10 Tips for Liking the Bible. This book rekindled my passion for reading the Bible. If you are a teacher, or an administrator - buy it. It will change your life!

Sheryl Nelson
School Director
City Kids School (Kirkland, WA)

In *10 Tips for Liking the Bible*, Keith coaches the reader with assurance, confidence, and strategy to turn from being a frustrated, obligated reader of God's Word to adopting a fresh experience with Scripture that is filled with joy. *10 Tips* is a vital resource with simple steps to help people at any stage in their relationship with Christ to grow in the critical spiritual discipline of reading and studying the Bible.

Matt Guevara
Campus Pastor
Christ Community Church (Bartlett, IL)

I recommend anything that Keith writes because he has a gift for helping others connect Truth to real life. When people apply his teaching, they will experience the right blend of head and heart!

Byron Emmert
Director of Leadership Development
Eagle Brook Church (Centerville, MN)

I really like the Bible! And, I really love the stories of God and His people. But, I could always use more tips on how to better engage, understand, and apply the Bible. *In 10 Tips for Liking the Bible*, Keith gives super practical tips that I am immediately putting into practice.

Amy Dolan
Children's Ministry Consultant at *Lemon Lime Kids* and
Curriculum Writer for *What's In the Bible?* (Chicago, IL)

Read. Reread. Repeat. Delighted readers will find themselves heeding author Keith Ferrin's instructions not only with God's Word, but also with his new book 10 Tips for Liking the Bible. Inspirational, yet practical, Ferrin compels us to dust off the pages of our Bibles as he condenses 20 years of experience sharing his love affair with God's word with audiences across America. Easy to read, insightful and results-oriented, people at all levels of faith will benefit from this book's wisdom. Enjoy it once, and then Read. Reread. Repeat.

Sarah Beckman
Salt and clay ministries (Albuquerque, NM)

For many, (especially students) the Bible can feel like a dull paperweight, a confusing movie, or a twisted instruction manual. Keith helped me flip that paradigm. In 10 Tips, he reminds us that the Bible is something we can actually like. It is written for me and to me from God. Keith simplifies what we so often complicate.

Peder Erik Brakke
Field StaffYoung Life (Redmond, WA)

As a family pastor, I have a strong desire for parents to fall in love with God's Word so they can share that love with their children. Keith's book is as an inspiring element to positively spur parents to appreciate the Bible in their lives. Hopefully, they will pass that appreciation on to the next generation.

Trevor Lee
Family Life Pastor, Life Community Church (Kirkland, WA)

Keith has done a great job of reminding us of some things we knew, providing us with some new thoughts, and debunking some well entrenched myths. His approach to approaching scripture is engaging, entertaining and enormously helpful. Thank-you my friend!

Curtis O. Fletcher
Senior Manager
Hitachi Consulting (Falcon, CO)

Keith Ferrin sits us down at the table of faith and plainly explains how to not simply read the Bible, but to dine on a five course meal with the creator of the Universe. **10 Tips for Liking the Bible** *invites us to push the crumbs aside and feast on all that God is offering.*

Krista Gilbert
Mother of four, writer, speaker, connector
(Coeur d'Alene, ID)

10 Tips for Liking the Bible *is the "user's guide" every Christian should have on their shelf. Keith Ferrin's honesty about the struggles many of us face and easy-to-apply tips help restore energy and passion to daily Bible reading.*

Tanya Divet
Blogger and teacher
(Fredericksburg VA)

Keith Ferrin's book *10 Tips for Liking the Bible* will inspire and encourage you to actively seek a deeper understanding of the living Word and point you towards a relationship with God like you have not yet encountered!

Rebecca Wells
Center Director
Turning Point Pregnancy Center (Scottsboro, AL)

Thank you for writing this special book. It has motivated me to read the Bible more and to love God's Word.

Debbie Fox
(Tifton, GA)

Keith Ferrin has given some very exciting ideas and strategies to use to read the Bible. I am very eager to use them to have a better understanding of the Bible. To hear God and talk to Him.

Tamara Lammers
Preschool Teacher/Director (Prior Lake, MN)

I have fallen in love with God's Word all over again reading this book. Not only did Keith bring the Word to life for me, but he brought God to life for me again! I will be forever grateful.

Nancy Stephens
(Parkersburg, WV)

10 Tips for Liking the Bible offers practical tips for life changing results that will have a huge impact on your personal relationship with God! Everyone should have a copy and put into practice the 10 tips.

Virginia Graves
Children's Director and mother of three daughters
(Maplewood, MN)

10 Tips for Liking the Bible is written both practically and vulnerably. Keith uses these tips to show just how the Word of God is living and active and in doing so brings enrichment to your relationship with God.

Brittany Lee Ketter
Blogger, ministry school student
(Pittsburgh, PA)

Ten Tips for Liking the Bible

(BECAUSE BELIEVING IT'S TRUE IS NOT ENOUGH)

Keith Ferrin

10 Tips for *Liking* the Bible

(Because Believing It's True Is Not Enough)

By Keith Ferrin

DEDICATION

This book is dedicated to Sarah, Caleb, and Hannah.

As you grow, may God's beautiful, mysterious, amazing story continue to engage you as deeply as it does today.

May you read it, trust it, internalize it, live it...and like it!

Love,
Dad

10 Tips for *Liking* the Bible

CONTENTS

10 TIPS FOR *LIKING* THE BIBLE

ACKNOWLEDGMENTS

This has been such a unique and cool project. What I thought was going to be a simple, short, eBook has turned into so much more. There are so many people who have either inspired this book, or had a hand directly in bringing it to fruition, that thanking them all by name would take way too many pages. I am talking about a couple hundred people. Seriously.

The "10 Tips Launch Team" – I have never had a launch team before. Now, I am not sure I will write another book without one. This was truly a team effort. You have read the manuscript again and again. You have found an embarrassing number of typos, grammatical errors, and places that simply needed to be cleaned up. You have provided invaluable insight on everything from the format, to the cover, to the landing page on my blog, to the study guide. The list goes on. Thank you. This has been heaps of fun!

Brian Gage – I always wait eagerly to see how you are going to take my words and ideas and turn them into a cover that conveys them both. And once again, you nailed it. I am thrilled to have you as my designer and even more grateful to say you're my friend.

To the readers of my blog and attendees of my presentations – You have made this book possible. You made comments on the blog, wrote me emails, shot me messages on Facebook, and spoke with me after presentations. The tips you told me were the most helpful for you are the ones that ended up in these pages. Thank you for your encouragement to keep writing and speaking. After almost twenty years, I still love it as much as ever. More, actually.

Kari – It is a joy to walk this road with you. We started dating the year I was internalizing the Gospel of John. We had no idea what God was up to. You were at my first presentation, only weeks before you walked down the aisle and took my name. You have walked beside me every day of this almost-two-decade journey. How about another five decades?

Sarah, Caleb, and Hannah – To see you fall more deeply in love with Jesus and His Word is truly one of the greatest joys of my life. You put up with your dad's crazy schedule with much more grace than I deserve. The best part of every trip is knowing that I get to come home to the coolest kids on the planet. And yes, we can read an extra story tonight.

INTRODUCTION

I didn't always like the Bible. Not that I disliked it. I didn't even *think* about liking it. Enjoying the Bible never really crossed my mind.

I spent the first twenty years I was a Christian believing that the Bible was true. Still do. Believing the Bible was reliable. Still believe that too. Believing that I should read it more, study it more deeply, and memorize more verses.

But the idea of *liking* it didn't even enter the conversation. In fact, I still rarely hear people talk about liking the Bible. It is almost as if we think that once we convince people it is true, reliable, and valuable, then they will read it every day, sign up for every Bible study, and memorize it cover to cover. (Ok...I might have just gone a bit too far.)

If you have ever heard me speak – or read one of my other books – you have heard me tell of the night I began to like the Bible. Yes, I can trace it back to a specific night in the spring of 1993.

A friend told me about an actor named Bruce Kuhn who was coming to his church to "perform" the Gospel of Luke. Bruce had memorized Luke. The whole book. And he got up on stage, quoted it, and acted it out at the same time. No sets. No props. No other actors or actresses.

Honestly, I went out of curiosity. I thought it would be fascinating, but I didn't expect to enjoy it. At least not for almost two hours! But that night, the living Word of God went from being a phrase to a reality. It came alive for me like never before. I sincerely enjoyed it. A lot!

Bruce agreed to have lunch with me the next day. We ended up spending about nine hours together. He challenged me to *hang out* in a book of the Bible. So I did.

That summer I read Philippians. Every day. All summer. It was the first time I could remember *liking* the Bible consistently for a long period of time. Thank you Bruce. I am forever grateful.

That was the summer of 1993. Just under three years later – in March of 1996 – I did my first presentation of the Gospel of John. I have spent the better part of the last two decades speaking, writing, and doing everything I can to help people fall in love with God's Word.

What you are about to read is my attempt to boil down the lessons, analogies, ideas, and habits people tell me have been the most helpful for them.

Ten tips. Ten tips that you can apply today. Ten tips that are simple to understand. Ten tips that are equally practical for the long-time Bible student or the person who is exploring what the big deal is about this old book.

The Bible is a big deal. (Check the all-time bestseller list. It's right at the top.)

Yes, it is true. Yes, it is practical. And yes, it is fun!

My goal is simple: To help you like the Bible. That's it. If you like it, you will read it more. If you like it, you will talk about it. If you like it, you will be more consistent in your time with God. If you like it, you will apply it.

When it comes to the Bible, God never intended you to stop at believing it is "true." He also wants you to *like* it. I do too.

So let's get started.

Alongside,
Keith

10 Tips for *Liking* the Bible

Tip 1

Remember Why You Are Doing This.

W hy do you read the Bible?

Take a moment to answer the question before moving on. (Hint: Your answer is *really* important.)

Whenever I ask this question – especially to a group of people sitting in a church – I typically get answers like this:

> *"It is an opportunity to know God's will."*

> *"I find encouragement there."*

> *"It is what I am supposed to do."*

> *"It reminds me of what is true."*

> *"It is how I know what God wants me to do."*

> *"It is God's Holy Word."*

All of these are true statements. Without a doubt. But once – just once – I would love to hear someone say, "I read it to hang out with God." I have yet to hear someone give that answer.

But isn't that the point? Isn't our time in God's Word primarily about spending time with Him? Being with Him. Knowing Him. Sitting with Him. Learning from Him. Laughing with Him. Hanging out with Him.

ONE OF MY PET PEEVES

It has been bugging me for almost twenty years now. I *wish* it had bugged me for longer. You see, we talk a lot about having a *relationship* with Jesus. (That's not the part that bugs me.) The part that really gets to me is *when* we talk about having a relationship with Jesus. Or even more specifically – when we *don't* talk about it.

We seem to talk about having a relationship right up to the time when someone actually says, "I'm in." Once someone is in the relationship, we stop talking about it. Odd...don't you think?

All too often, the conversation moves pretty quickly to church attendance, volunteering, joining a small group, or reading the Bible to learn about God.

Don't get me wrong. Every one of these is a good and necessary practice. But notice the last three words of the previous paragraph: "learn about God." Isn't the goal of a relationship to *know* someone, not know *about* them?

In John 14-16, we are given a peek into a very intimate scene. Jesus has shared a meal with the twelve guys He has traveled with for the past three years. One of them left the meal...to betray Him. The rest have gone out for a walk. This is His last conversation with them before the worst night and day of His life.

As you might expect, He is talking about things that really matter. Bearing fruit. Staying connected. Enduring suffering. Receiving the Holy Spirit. Having peace. Overcoming the world. (You know...big stuff.)

Smack dab in the middle of this conversation, Jesus says these words:

"I no longer call you servants, because a servant does not know his master's business. Instead, I have called you friends, for everything that I learned from my Father I have made known to you." (John 15: 15, NIV)

Friends. That is what Jesus called them. Not servants. Not partners in business. Not workers or team members or helpers. *Friends.*

Oh, how our time in the Bible would change if we kept the friendship front and center. If our time in God's Word was primarily relational, instead of informational, then it would have a significantly higher probability of being transformational!

Is there information in the Bible? *Yes.* Do we learn some things about God in His Word? *Yes.* Does spending time in the Bible lead to a better understanding of God, His will, and His ways? *Yes, yes,* and *yes.*

But the context of that information is the relationship. The umbrella under which all that information sits is the relationship.

So...how do we keep the focus on the relationship? (I'm glad you asked.) Hopefully, these two pictures will help.

PICTURE ONE: YOU, GOD, AND A CUP OF COFFEE.

Imagine that you recently moved to my hometown near Seattle. Some friends introduce us. We find we have a lot in common. With a desire to get to know each other better, we decide to meet at a local coffee shop once a week before work.

TIP 1: REMEMBER WHY YOU ARE DOING THIS.

Over the course of the next several weeks, would you and I learn some information about each other? Absolutely. We would most likely learn about our families, what brought you to Seattle, where we grew up, what we do for work, our likes and dislikes, and a wide range of other information.

Now, rewind just a minute and imagine that I show up the first week with a notepad in hand. I sit down, take a sip of coffee, pick up my pen, and you notice that across the top of the notepad I have written:

> "82 THINGS I NEED TO KNOW ABOUT JOE
> FOR HIM TO BE MY FRIEND."

Then I start asking you questions about your family, job, etc. The information I would get would likely be the *same information* I would learn if we just sat and talked. But how different would it feel? More importantly, what would be the chance of you showing up the next week? Zero.

But don't we do that to God all the time?

We sit down, open our Bibles, grab whatever devotional book we happen to be reading, and begin looking for the "answers" to today's questions. Once we have read the passage and filled in the answers, we must be done. Right?

Doesn't sound very relational. Sometimes, I think we walk away from our time with God without ever having been *with* God at all! I wonder how frequently I check off my Had-A-Quiet-Time checkbox and God is thinking, "Hey Keith. I'd still like to hang out with you a bit. I'm not finished."

Ouch.

Picture Two: Playing with God.

Some days God wants you to read the Bible and not *learn* anything.

That may sound a little strange coming from someone who writes and speaks about studying the Bible for a living. Stick with me for a few more paragraphs and you'll see what I mean.

My wife, Kari, and I have three kids. There are days – or parts of days – when I need to teach my kids something. Other days I need to discipline them. Still others require that I correct them, encourage them, comfort them, or even inspire them to be more than they would otherwise be on their own.

There are also days when we just play catch. Or ride bikes. Or bake cookies. (Ok...Kari does the baking with them. I do the Quality Assurance Testing.)

Here's the deal: Those days when we only play together are *not* less valuable! In many ways, they are more valuable than the days of instruction and correction.

Could you imagine the expressions on Sarah's, Caleb's, and Hannah's faces if Kari and I sat them down, looked them in the eyes, and I said,

> *"Your mother and I have decided there is just too much to teach you. Too much you need to be corrected on, instructed about, and yes, even some occasional comforting. Because of this, we have decided we will do no more playing. You three can play with each other and your friends. But we are here to teach, discipline, and comfort you. Off you go."*

TIP 1: REMEMBER WHY YOU ARE DOING THIS.

I can hear the thoughts in your head. *"No way." "That's insane." "How can you give up playing with your kids?" "That's not a relationship at all."*

Aha. Not a relationship at all.

And yet, so often, that is how I tend to view God. When I pick up the Bible I am supposed to learn something, get corrected, be inspired, or read some comforting words. Of course there are days when these things happen. But hear this clearly: Sometimes God wants you to pick up His Word and just enjoy the read.

I remember talking to a friend one time who is an actor and director. He told me of a conversation he had years earlier with an older, British director. Their conversation was about whether the Bible could hold its own on stage with some of the great theater productions. Not whether it was true, but whether it was *good theater*. After a few minutes, this older man said [insert British accent here]:

> *"Well, you know...the Bible is the Word of Almighty God. But it also happens to be a jolly good read!"*

Amen.

God has much to teach us. We have much to learn. But don't miss the story. It is such a fantastic story! There are heroes, battles, and villains. There are crazy characters, and yes, some dull ones. There are plot twists, mystery, and intrigue. There is humor. Lots of it. I'm not kidding. (Pun intended. Forgive me.)

One of my favorite things about presenting the Gospel of John is watching how frequently the audience laughs. They don't expect to. But they do. Every time.

After all, what is the *story* of the gospels? Aren't they four accounts of thirteen guys on a three-year road trip? Have you ever been on a road trip? Funny stuff happens.

Not only that, but the most serious, biblical scholars will tell you that at least a handful of the disciples were teenagers. Have you ever been on a road trip with teenagers?! As someone who spent six years as a youth pastor, I can assure you that laughter is part of the deal.

Even after two decades of telling these stories, it is so easy for me to go back to simply gleaning information from the pages of Scripture, rather than being engulfed by the story. I have to constantly remind myself: *It is about the relationship.*

Relationship. Relationship. Relationship.

You will be tempted to go back to information. Don't do it.

Each time you sit down to hang out with God in His Word, get one – or both – of these pictures in your mind. You and God sitting down for a cup of coffee. God as a Daddy who wants to play with you. As your mindset shifts from information to relationship, you will find that you are more likely to be ready on the days when God *does* want to teach you something, inspire you, discipline you, or comfort you.

And you will find that you like the Bible, and the Author, more than ever before.

Tip 2

*Set Your Expectations
Really High.*

Think about the last party you went to. See the people. Taste the food. Hear the conversations, the laughter...or the arguments.

If you can, rewind all the way to *before* you arrived at the party. What was your expectation? Did you expect it to be fun? Did you expect it to be boring? If you went to the party expecting it to be fun – did you have a good time? If you went expecting it to be boring – did you spend most of the evening figuring out a way to duck out early? (Yeah...I've been there.)

YOUR EXPECTATIONS MAKE A MASSIVE DIFFERENCE.

Certainly there are times when expectations are wonderfully exceeded or fall woefully short. Typically though, that is the exception, not the rule. It is much more common to have our expectation and experience line up pretty closely.

If you go to a movie expecting it to be funny, it is highly probable that you will find yourself laughing. If you enter a meeting with your boss expecting it to go poorly, the chance of it going well is not too high. If you expect to not like a new food your parents set before you, well...ask my three kids how that goes.

When it comes to the Bible, the same rule applies. Your expectations make a massive difference. Sadly, most of us expect the Bible to be *true*, but we don't expect to *like* it.

As I wrote in the last chapter, we might expect to learn something, be challenged, get corrected, or even receive some comfort. But laugh, cry, or be drawn into the story so deeply that we glance at the clock only to realize we have read *longer* than we intended? Not usually.

So let me ask you a question...

WHAT IS YOUR EXPECTATION WHEN YOU OPEN YOUR BIBLE?

You have expectations when you open your Bible. We all do. They might be high. Or, if you are like many of the people who speak with me after a presentation or send me an email, your expectations are probably pretty low. And if you don't expect to like the Bible, guess what? You won't.

That might sound pretty harsh. But please, please remember, I am someone who spent the first twenty years of my Christian life believing the Bible was true. I just didn't like it very much. Looking back, I am convinced that much of it had to do with my expectation.

It wasn't until I was in my mid-20's – after seeing Bruce Kuhn "perform" the Gospel of Luke – that my expectation changed. After that night, I started expecting the Bible to be good. I expected it to be funny, engaging, and enjoyable. Let me tell you, when it comes to my love for God's Word, the last two decades have been much better than the first two!

Take a few minutes and be honest about your own expectations of the Bible. Spend some time talking with God about it. If your expectations are low, tell Him. You are not going to disappoint Him. He already knows.

After sharing your honest expectations with God, let me remind you of something...

YOU CAN CHANGE YOUR EXPECTATIONS.

You don't have to stay where you are. The Bible can be exciting and enjoyable for you. It is possible to have David's words be your own:

*The law of the Lord is perfect, refreshing the
soul.
The statutes of the Lord are trustworthy,
making wise the simple.
The precepts of the Lord are right, giving joy to
the heart.
The commands of the Lord are radiant, giving
light to the eyes.
The fear of the Lord is pure, enduring forever.
The decrees of the Lord are firm, and all of
them are righteous.
They are more precious than gold, than much
pure gold;
They are sweeter than honey, than honey from
the honeycomb.* (Psalm 19:8-10, NIV)

David loved the Bible. You can too.

However, if your expectations are going to change, you
must *choose* to change them. The Holy Spirit will certainly aid
in that process. But He will not force it. After all, if time in
God's Word is primarily *relational*, then both parties have to
want to be there. Forcing you to enjoy it makes no sense.

The next time you pick up your Bible, check your
expectation first. Pause for a moment and say (maybe even out
loud),

> *"God, I am really looking forward to this. I am
> excited to be with You as I read Your Word. I
> look forward to hearing Your voice today. I*

don't know all that You have in store for me,
but I eagerly await what You have planned.
Use this time to draw me closer to Your heart,
to Your joy, to Your peace, to Your hope, and
to You."

Set your expectations high. Really high! After all, we are talking about the unfathomable privilege of reading words written by the Author of Life! The One who invented words. The One who created your heart, knows you intimately, and loves you deeply. Then watch what happens.

As with any habit, making the choice to change is the hardest step. The irony is that the more you take time to intentionally set your expectations, the less you will have to be intentional about it. You will find yourself looking forward to the next time you get to read the Bible. And when "have to read the Bible" changes to "get to read the Bible," I guess you won't really need this book anymore!

10 Tips for *Liking* the Bible

Tip 3

Have A Strategy.

T here is one question I have asked literally hundreds of times to thousands of people. The response is *always* the same. Sighs are heavy. Eyes are rolled. Hands are raised. The question?

> *Is there anyone here who struggles with their mind wandering when they read the Bible?*

Excuse me, did you just let out a heavy sigh?

I meet very few people who *don't* struggle with this. The Wandering Mind is something I have battled against for as long as I can remember. Not just when I was young. Throughout my teens, into my 20's and beyond, the struggle has been present on a daily basis.

One morning it all came to a head. I was so frustrated. I had been a Christian for 25 years. I had already internalized Philippians, the Gospel of John, and II Timothy. I had been presenting the Gospel of John for a couple years. I *knew* how awesome the Bible could be.

And yet, I couldn't get more than two or three paragraphs into the Bible without my mind drifting off into space. I simply could not focus. And I was mad.

This is the conversation I had with God after closing my Bible in frustration.

> Me: "God...What is wrong with me? Why can't I focus? I love You. I love Your Word. I know it is alive. But it doesn't feel alive. Why is it that I can read a novel for two hours without having my mind drift at all, but I can't read two

paragraphs of the Bible without thinking of a million different things?"

God: *"Excuse me. Can I talk now?"*

Me: *"Er...um...ok..."*

The following dream/analogy/vision popped into my head. (I know this might be scary, but go with me into my brain.)

> *I was a running back on a football team. My team was on the 20-yard line. Eighty yards to go. My number was called. I was getting the ball.*
>
> *I had prepared. I had practiced. I was in shape. I had studied the playbook. I knew where the hole was going to be and what blockers to follow. And I had done that all-important task of "visualizing the end zone." I could already hear the crowd cheering.*
>
> *The quarterback handed me the ball and off I went. Three yards...on my way...ten yards...wahoo!...twenty-two yards.... BLAM!*
>
> *Flat on my back.*
>
> *Hmmmm...Why am I not in the end zone? I visualized the end zone. I want to be in the end zone. Why am I not in the end zone?!*
>
> *A teammate came over to help me up and heard me mumbling those questions to myself. He simply responded, "Hey man. It might have something to do with the guys playing defense."*

Did you catch that? I had never even *thought* about it. Every time you and I sit down to read our Bibles there is someone playing defense. Someone who is actively trying to make sure we don't like it. Someone who is throwing distractions our way.

And the "defense" starts early. It starts before you even pick up your Bible. Have you ever heard any of these?

"You don't have time to read the Bible."

"It won't make a difference anyway."

"There are more important things to do."

"You need that extra thirty minutes of sleep way more than you need time with God."

And it continues as we read. Distractions. Random thoughts. Even important things that need to be thought about, but could wait till later.

For years, every time I would get distracted, I would simply blame myself. Thoughts like:

"Why can't I focus?"

"Why don't I like the Bible?"

"I don't think I'll ever get better at this."

"I should just quit."

Where do those thoughts sound like they come from? Anyone who has ever played sports will tell you that as soon as you can get the other team down on themselves, your work is done. Game over.

Bottom Line: We need a strategy for beating the defense. By far, the best strategy is prayer.

This is not a simple, two-second *"Help me focus"* prayer. This is strategic prayer. In fact, there are three specific times when prayer will help you "beat the defense."

PRAY BEFORE YOU EVER OPEN YOUR BIBLE.

I don't encourage you to start with prayer because it is the "Christian" thing to do. I put it first because it is truly the most important. Going back to *Tip 1*, if we are going to shift from informational Bible study to relational Bible study, it is probably not a bad idea to begin by chatting with God.

There are three prayers I pray before I ever start reading. Each helps get me in the right mindset as I prepare to read.

God, Thank You for Your Living Word.

It is easier to focus on something that we are grateful for, as opposed to something we feel obligated to. This is a simple prayer, but an important one nonetheless.

The God of the universe has given you His Word. He is talking with you. He wrote these words centuries ago – with you in mind! This isn't simply a textbook to be studied. It is a poem, a letter, a novel, a guidebook, a biography, and an autobiography...all rolled up together. And it is for you. Starting with a thankful heart will keep you engaged as you read.

God, What do You want to do today?

As you have likely gathered by now, time in God's Word is primarily a relational activity – not an informational one. For many of us, we have spent years studying the Bible informationally. It is now a habit to approach the Bible with a mindset that says, *God, what do You want to teach me today?*

What if God doesn't want to teach you anything? What if He just wants to hang out with you? What if he wants to encourage you, comfort you, or simply remind you that He has been in relationships with a lot of messy people (just like you and me) for a very long time?

We have already explored this, but it bears repeating: Some days God most certainly will want to teach you something. Just not *every* day. If you have either been a parent or had parents, you know this intuitively. Some days my dad taught me stuff. Then there were days when we just played catch. Both were necessary.

Asking this question helps us approach our time in the Bible conversationally. After all, would you be able to stay focused on a conversation with a friend who *only* wanted to teach you things every time you got together? You would quickly get bored. Then you would stop getting together. Sounds like my pattern of Bible reading the first twenty years.

God, Help me focus.

Sounds simple, doesn't it? But doesn't it make sense? To continue the football analogy from earlier, if someone is playing defense, aren't we better off with blockers? So frequently we forget that God has angels prepared to help us. (See Hebrews 1:14.)

TIP 3: HAVE A STRATEGY.

No running back would ever step on the field without bringing his teammates along. If the enemy is actively trying to make sure that we don't enjoy our time in God's Word, why would we ever try to fight that fight on our own? What chance do we stand? But, if God's angels are blocking for us, that's another story.

Next time you reach for your Bible, pause for a few minutes and pray these three prayers. You will be surprised how much easier it is to focus – and how much more you enjoy it.

PAUSE TO PRAY WHILE YOU ARE READING.

Again – this is not rocket science – but it is so frequently left out.

Here is a common scenario: I begin reading. Two paragraphs in and my mind is off who-knows-where. I tell myself, "Okay, Keith. You are going to focus. You can do it. Focus." This typically works for about two more paragraphs. About the third time I have this conversation with myself, I am pretty frustrated. Might even put the Bible down and chalk this one up to a bad day of time in God's Word. I'll try again tomorrow.

Really? A "bad day?"

Back to the running back analogy. I have *never* seen a running back get tackled a few times and then simply walk off, mid-way through the first quarter, and chalk it up to a "bad day" on the field. He might be frustrated. He certainly didn't *want* to get tackled.

What I usually see is a running back on the sidelines, talking with the coach. Making plans for the next time he goes out on the field. New strategies for beating the defense. Maybe even a quick pep talk. This all takes place *in the middle of the game.*

Now, when I find my mind wandering, I stop and talk to the Coach. When I do, I am reminded of three truths:

The Coach is on my side.

I am not alone in this. You are not alone in this. God is pulling for you. He is on your side. He wants your time in His Word to be beneficial and enjoyable. Knowing that God is for you – instead of disappointed in you – is an enormous encouragement as you begin reading again.

The Coach knows how to beat the defense.

God has been at this a long time. He knows all of the enemy's tricks. He is not surprised by any of it. When we pause to talk to God, share our frustrations, and ask for help, He is more than happy to give it...without blame or shame. (See James 1:5) He will remind us of His presence. He will send "blockers" to keep distractions away.

The Coach sometimes just wants to chat.

Most of the time, my prayer in the middle of reading is quite short. Often less than a minute. But there are times when I never get back to my Bible reading. I spend time talking with God. And listening to God. (Arguably more important than the talking part.) Even when my intention is to spend 30-45 minutes reading the Bible, if I end up reading for five minutes, and chatting with God the rest of the time, that is *not* time poorly spent!

TIP 3: HAVE A STRATEGY.

Before moving on, I want to make it clear that my mind *still* wanders sometimes. Even at times right after I have been talking with the Coach. That is when I pause, chat with the Coach again and get back at it. After all, I have yet to meet a running back who figured out a way to never get tackled. Even so, they always want to get back in the game.

PRAY AFTER YOU CLOSE YOUR BIBLE.

This may seem like an odd strategy when the goal is to keep your mind from wandering *while* you are reading the Bible. Maybe this will help...

Have you ever had one of those projects at work- or classes in school - where you couldn't stop thinking about it when you were away from it? When you returned, how focused were you? Did you have to *work* at keeping your mind from wandering? Probably not.

> *The more you think about something while you are away from it, the easier it is to focus when you return.*

So often we set aside time to read or pray. But that's just it. We "set aside" time to read or pray. It is designated time, not a practice that permeates our lives. Seems I read something somewhere about praying *continually*. (See I Thess. 5:16-18.)

If we want to be able to focus while we read, we have got to be in conversation with God when we are *not reading*. Those conversations will develop our hunger for the Word. A longing to get back to the Word. To continue the conversation as we read.

It is essential to spend some time in prayer immediately after reading the Bible. As I am wrapping up my time in the Word I pray a prayer similar to this:

> *"Lord Jesus, help me remember what I have read here this morning. Let's talk about this again throughout the day. Bring it to my mind as I have periods of down time. When I'm driving my car, eating my lunch, or brushing my teeth. Remind me of Your Word as I face situations where Your Word would bring needed comfort, a helpful reminder, valuable instruction, or even necessary correction. Let your Word saturate my thoughts and attitudes."*

It is also crucial to pray at any and every other time. I know, I know. Sounds like a good, Sunday School answer. But how often do we ignore the times when God actually answers the first prayer? He brings something to mind and we don't engage in the conversation He is starting. We will gladly pick up our mobile phone for anyone who happens to call at any random time. But when God calls? Too busy. He couldn't really be talking to me. I am imagining this.

What would happen if we prayed that God would talk to us throughout the day, expected that He would, and then engaged in the conversations when He did? Those conversations would become easier, more frequent, more enjoyable, and more fruitful. We would become shaped by them. We would look forward to them.

And when we returned to the Bible? We wouldn't struggle as much with our wandering mind, because we would *anticipate* meeting Jesus there. And indeed we would.

Pray before reading your Bible. Pray in the middle. Pray after. It might sound simple, but in this case, simple is exactly what is needed most.

Tip 4

Watch The Whole Movie.

I love movies. And I am not really picky. Action movies. *Of course.* Comedies. *Who doesn't like them?* Intense thrillers? *The more twists the better.* Cheesy romantic comedies. *Guilty.*

Now, picture this scene. Kari and I have invited you and a few other friends over to watch a movie. You find a cozy spot on the couch. Your feet land on the ottoman only moments before your hand lands in the popcorn bowl. You grin as you realize your fingertips are now coated with that heavenly blend of butter and salt. I push "Play" and a couple minutes later the opening credits dissolve into Scene One. As the scene comes to a close, I push "Pause" and say, "Let's discuss this before watching Scene Two." You politely participate in the awkward conversation and a few minutes later, I push "Play." At the end of Scene Two, I do it again. And again after Scene Three. Watch...Pause...Discuss. Watch...Pause...Discuss.

How much would you enjoy that evening? Actually, since we are pausing to discuss every scene, watching the movie will need to be spread out over the next eight Friday nights. Two months will pass before the final credits roll.

This might sound completely absurd, but don't we do the very same thing to the Bible all the time? We decide we are going to study a book of the Bible and so we break it down into small pieces. We look at one piece, discuss it, and then do the same with the next piece. We never sit down and just read it.

IF YOU WANT TO LIKE THE BIBLE, YOU HAVE TO READ *MORE* OF IT.

Stop for a second and think of your favorite novelist. This author has just come out with a new book. You pick up a copy and immediately dive in. But wait a second. What if I said you could only read one page a day? How much would you like that book? Take this one step further. What if you could only read a couple paragraphs each day? Would it even be possible to get through it? Not likely.

We wouldn't even think about reading a novel that way. And yet, when I ask people how they read the Bible, by far the most common answers I get are:

"I read a chapter a day."

"I read whatever is in my devotional."

Do you realize that the average chapter of the Bible takes less than four minutes to read? The average section of Scripture in a devotional book takes about thirty seconds! Can you think of *anything* that you can read for thirty seconds to four minutes a day and truly enjoy? (Ok...maybe the comics, but I can't think of anything else.)

Not only that, but it simply doesn't make sense to only read a little at a time. Let's use Philippians to show you what I mean. It probably wouldn't be a huge revelation if I told you that Philippians is a four-chapter letter, written by the Apostle Paul, to the Church in Philippi. Now, imagine that you went out to your mailbox and tucked in the middle of the pizza coupons, bills, and credit card offers was an envelope with your name handwritten on the outside. In the corner was the name of someone you love whom you haven't seen in a few years. Inside you find a four-page, handwritten letter. The letter starts out,

> *Dear Elizabeth, I thank my God every time I remember you. Every time I pray for you, I pray with joy.*

Would you read page one and say, "That is enough for today. I better save page two for tomorrow. Four days from now, I'll finish this up."

Not a chance. You would read it, realize you are still standing by your mailbox, go inside, and read it again! So why don't we do that with Philippians? That's how Philippians starts. It is a letter. A letter from someone who loves and misses his friends. A letter about joy in the midst of struggle. A letter written with a deep sense of gratitude and partnership. How often we miss it because we are too busy "studying" it.

Please, please don't hear what I am not saying! I am not saying you should never study a chapter, paragraph, or even meditate on a single word or phrase. What I am saying is that detailed study is not the place to start. Talking about a single scene, character, or plot twist in a movie is valuable and enjoyable. But only *after* you have seen the movie. (We will explore this in a bit more detail in *Tip 9*.)

Next time you pick up your Bible, sit down and read a whole book. More than half of the sixty-six books in the Bible can be read in less than thirty minutes. Pick one of those. Try Philippians, II Timothy, James, or I Peter. Reading at an average, the-way-you-would-talk pace, you will finish in less than twenty minutes. And you will reap some fantastic benefits.

YOU WILL EASILY ENTER THE STORY.

Give it a try. Reading more will trigger something in your brain. You will start to see the characters, hear their voices, and visualize the events. It won't take a lot of extra effort. It will just happen.

Here's the proof. Remember the last time you saw a movie *after* reading the book on which the movie was based? What was your reaction? If you are anything like me, you probably had to force yourself to keep from yelling at the screen.

> *"Hey! Did the casting director even read the book? She was taller. He had darker hair. They lived in San Francisco, not San Diego!"*

Now, try to recall the last time you started a novel but got pulled away after only a couple pages. What did you do when you returned to the book? I bet you didn't start on Page 3. Of course not. You started at the beginning, because the last time you never got into it.

The same can – and will – happen with the Bible. When we read more of it, we easily get into it. When we read little bits, we don't. It is as simple as that.

YOU WILL REMEMBER WHAT YOU READ.

Have you ever read the Bible in the morning, gone on with the rest of your day, and then couldn't remember what you read when someone asked you about it later in the day? You remember sitting down with your Bible and your cup of coffee.

You remember what chair you sat in. You remember what time it was when you started and ended. But no matter how hard you tried, you couldn't remember *what* you read. Ugh. Talk about frustrating!

When you read a whole book of the Bible – or a large chunk of a longer book – you will be tapping into how your brain naturally and easily learns anything. Yes...*anything*. Our brains learn from the big to the small. The reverse is also true. Our brains do *not* learn easily from the small to the big. Looking at details first never leads to long term memory.

> *Put another way: Our brains learn in the context of story.*

Try this. Think of something you know really well. Something you could explain in broad terms or great detail. It might be your favorite sport. Maybe some aspect of your job. Could be music or plumbing or oceanography or painting or entering dog shows.

Got it? Now, how did you *first* learn about it? Did someone sit you down and teach you one tiny detail? Or did they sit with you and watch a game, take you to a concert, or visit an aquarium?

One example I frequently use is soccer. While soccer is a growing sport in the United States (where I live), it certainly is nowhere near as popular as football, basketball, or baseball. Typically, when I ask an audience how many people have played a lot of soccer, about 5-10% of hands will go up.

If I sat down with the folks who raised their hands, we could jump into a detailed conversation about the strategy of a flat defense versus an arched defense versus a diamond defense. In competitive soccer, this is an important concept to understand and know when to apply.

That said...there is a 90-95% chance that the words of that last paragraph sounded to you like the adults in a Charlie Brown® cartoon. Mwaah, Mwaah, Mwaah, Mwaah...

It would be much better for me to start with, "There are eleven guys on one side. Eleven guys on the other. Get the ball in the net on the opposite end of the field. By the way – no hands!" After that, we can break it down to offense, midfielders, defense, and goalies. Much, much later we can have detailed conversations about the techniques and strategies of each. Is the detail important? *Yes.* Is it the starting point? *No way.*

The same holds true with the Bible. When you start by looking at one paragraph or one chapter, you are trying to force your brain to take in the content in a way that it wasn't designed to take it in. When you "watch the movie" you will remember it. The story will stick. The context will be set as a foundation. After that foundation has been laid, it will always be present, making the detailed study a deeper discussion of a story you already know.

WHAT ABOUT THE LONGER BOOKS?

I get this question all the time. As I mentioned earlier, a majority of the sixty-six books of the Bible can be read in less than thirty minutes. That still leaves twenty-five to thirty books that can't be read in one sitting. Unless you have four hours every day, you are not going to be able to apply this when you study Genesis. In cases like these, here is what I recommend:

Read for an amount of time...
not an amount of chapters.

Reading for an amount of time puts you in a very different mindset than reading an amount of chapters. For example, if you decide to read <u>six chapters</u>, your mindset at the end of each chapter will be, "I have five/four/three more chapters to get through." If you set aside <u>thirty minutes</u> to read (more than enough time for six chapters), your mindset will shift to, "I still get to read for fifteen more minutes." That shift from "get through" to "get to" is huge.

So, decide beforehand how much time you have. When I ask, most people tell me they have fifteen, twenty, or thirty minutes. Let's take the middle time – twenty minutes – and apply that to reading a long book – the Gospel of John.

Reading at an average pace, the Gospel of John takes just about two hours. Since it has twenty-one chapters, if I read using the Chapter-A-Day method, it will take me three weeks. (And that's if I never miss a day!) However, if I simply decide to read for twenty minutes each day, I will read the whole book three-and-a-half times in that same three-week period.

How much more will I remember if I go with the second option? Not only that, but how much more will I *like it*?

I have said it before, but it is too important not to repeat: Our brains learn naturally and easily in the context of story. The only way we are going to understand the Story, remember the Story, and enjoy the Story is by reading the Story. The whole thing. In one sitting whenever possible.

Tip 5

*Learn From Your
Shampoo Bottle.*

Astory is told of the CEO of a toiletries company who wanted to foster creativity throughout his company. He sent out a memo inviting anyone at any level in the company to submit ideas for how to increase sales. Any employee whose idea showed demonstrable, positive impact would receive a small percentage of the profits.

Ideas came in. Some good. Some less than good. The CEO was intrigued when one of the factory workers came in and simply said, "I have an idea that will cost almost nothing and will increase sales by 40-70%." The CEO raised a disbelieving eyebrow and asked the man to elaborate. He simply picked up a shampoo bottle, pointed at the directions, and said, "Add the word 'repeat.' Lather. Rinse. Repeat."

I have searched, and haven't been able to prove – or disprove – the veracity of this story. (But I sure hope it's true.) A version of it has made its way into at least one novel, _The Plagiarist_ by Benjamin Cheever. Either way, look on the back of almost any shampoo bottle and you will see it. *Repeat.*

We will benefit greatly if we apply the same principle to Bible reading. In the last tip, I made the argument that reading whole books will help you remember what you read. Let's keep that theme going.

WHAT GETS REPEATED GETS REMEMBERED.

We don't need to spend a long time on this one because you intuitively – and experientially – know it to be true. Let me ask you:

TIP 5: LEARN FROM YOUR SHAMPOO BOTTLE.

Have you ever been listening to the radio and had a song come on you haven't heard in over a decade? Were you singing along by the second line?

Do you recall any old addresses or phone numbers?

Can you finish any of these sentences?

- M&Ms: *Melts in your mouth, not _____.*
- Rolaids: *How do you spell _____?*
- Dodge: *Dodge trucks are _____ tough.*
- Smith Barney: *We make money the old-fashioned way, we _____ _____.*
- The Energizer Bunny: *He keeps _____ and _____ and _____.*

How many of you parents out there have VeggieTales® songs in your head that you wish would go away? (Even though your kids are now in college!)

Not too long ago, I was speaking to the student body at Moody Bible Institute in Chicago. In an effort to make this same point, I simply said, "Finish this sentence: Hello. My name is Inigo Montoya..." The point was made when 1,500 college students yelled back: "...you killed my father. Prepare to die!" (Side Note: If you have never seen the 1987 film *The Princess Bride* you owe it to yourself to watch it. Soon. Life-changing. Not *Schindler's List* life-changing. More like silly-and-super-funny-with-heaps-of-quotable-lines life-changing.)

I asked how many of them had ever *tried* to memorize that line. Of course, no one raised a hand. (One class clown up in the balcony shouted out. But I haven't been able to track him down.) They didn't need to memorize it. In the movie he says it six times. Most of those students have seen the whole movie at least six times. After hearing it thirty-six times, it was in there!

One last thing before we move on to the next benefit. When these students shouted the ending of the movie line – they used an accent! A few of them even shouted out some other lines. When I asked them if they could picture Inigo chasing the six-fingered man through the house, there was laughter and hoots of affirmation.

Why? Because the last tip and this tip go hand in hand.

I ended the last chapter by saying that our brains learn naturally and easily in the context of story. The *context* is story, but the *process* is repetition. We learn in the context of story by the process of repetition.

REPETITION WILL LEAD TO MORE FREQUENT CONVERSATIONS WITH GOD.

We began this whole journey together by remembering that Bible reading is about the relationship. This might sound obvious, but the relationship doesn't end when you close your Bible. Ideally, our time in God's Word should foster conversations with God throughout the day. This will happen if repetition is built into your Bible reading.

When you "soak" in the same section of Scripture for days – or weeks – at a time, God will weave it in and through your daily life. He will bring to mind an encouraging passage when frustration or discouragement rears its head. At just the right moment, when you don't know what to say to a friend, God will remind you of the promise you read that morning. When your eyes and mind go where they shouldn't go, He will gently

– or not so gently – shake you and remind you where your focus should be.

This has truly been one of the most beneficial and enjoyable changes I have seen in my own Bible reading over the last twenty years. The Bible is no longer just "something I do" early in the morning. It is part of a conversation that *starts* early in the morning and *continues* throughout the day. That didn't happen until I committed to staying with one book, story, or Psalm – sometimes for weeks at a time.

REPETITION IS THE PRECURSOR TO ENJOYING DETAILED STUDY.

I understand that not every reader is a sports fan, but allow me to revisit the soccer analogy for a couple paragraphs. I truly enjoy talking about the intricacies of soccer. I love exploring ideas for teaching new skills and strategies to the girls on my daughter's team (which I have coached the last few years). It is fun for me to dialogue with other Seattle Sounders' fans about the fantastic plays and the failed attempts from the previous match.

The same is *not* true for every sport, or even every soccer team. I don't have a basic knowledge of every sport. I haven't watched every professional soccer team. I am not familiar with their strengths, weaknesses, players, or coaches. If I acquired a basic knowledge of a sport or team, then I would be ready to have a more detailed conversation.

For many of us, we put detailed study of the Bible *ahead* of general understanding. Then we wonder why we don't like it more. We try to figure out what Philippians 4:13 means without being able to say what Philippians is about. We have discussions about what Paul meant when he said, "I have fought the good fight, I have finished the race, I have kept the faith." (II Timothy 4:7) At the same time, we don't even know that Paul writes those words from Death Row, just weeks or months before he is executed. If someone asked us, "What is II Timothy about?" all we could offer is a blank stare.

There is a solution. Read. Reread. Repeat. You might not think you could ever love meditating on a single paragraph or doing a word study. If either of those is your *starting point*, I would agree with you. But if you read the book or section over and over until it was a part of you first? I guarantee you that your deeper study would be much more enjoyable.

I imagine that you enjoy having deep conversations with friends you know well. I bet you can easily remember a multi-hour conversation over coffee. Recalling a time when a small group of friends shared struggles, prayed for each other, and even wept with each other probably isn't a difficult task.

Now, imagine that someone you *didn't* know tried to have one of those conversations with you. The first time you met! Talk about awkward. Frankly, it would be inappropriate. It isn't time to go that deep. Not yet. But once you know each other. Once you have history. Once you can carry that relational history into the conversation. Then it is time. That is when the deep, intimate conversation becomes not only appropriate, but wonderful!

The same is true with the Bible. After you have repeatedly read a section, deep study becomes like that intimate conversation. The whole story stays with you. You don't forget the big picture just because you are focusing on a small section. That's like saying you would forget what a movie is about because you are having a conversation about a single scene. That makes no sense. Having a conversation about a single scene is actually enjoyable – provided you have seen the movie!

HOW MANY TIMES SHOULD I READ AND REREAD?

The short answer is: Until you know it. The slightly longer answer is: It depends on how long a book is, what genre it is, and how well you want to know it.

For shorter books that I am planning to study deeply and internalize, my general rule is "30 Times In 30 Days." Take a short book – like Philippians or II Timothy – and read it every day for a month. Watch what happens. After a week, you will notice that you simply *feel* differently about it than you did before. You will start to see the characters as real people. You will picture them and hear their voices. After a month, you will be more than ready to dive in deeper. (More on the day-by-day process in *Tip* 9.)

With Psalms and Proverbs, I like to take one at a time instead of reading the whole book. In my opinion, the more poetic genres are meant to be read and experienced more than picked apart. My favorite thing to do is to take a Psalm and simply read it each morning and evening for a few days or a week. Then go on to the next one. You can certainly do the same thing with Proverbs. I have met many people who read one Proverb a day. Since there are thirty-one, they end up reading the whole book a dozen times every year.

To read a longer book thirty times would take quite a while. I don't have a set rule for longer books. My approach really goes back to something Bruce Kuhn said to me in 1993, the day after I first saw him present the Gospel of Luke. We were having lunch and I asked him how he went about memorizing (I hadn't started using the word *internalizing* yet) the whole Gospel of Luke. He simply said,

> *"Memorize the story first. Then use the words
> on the page to tell the story."*

Those words have stuck with me for twenty years now. Today I give you the same advice: Memorize the story first. With a longer book – like Genesis or one of the gospels – read it until you know the story. Read it until you could walk someone through the book without leaving any of the stories out. Read it until the story, the rhythm, and the flow becomes a part of you.

At that point, you will *want* to go deeper. So dive in.

Tip 6

Raise Your Voice.

Back in *Tip 3*, I said that prayer is the Number One strategy for "beating the defense." While prayer is the Number One strategy, it isn't the only strategy. There is another strategy that has become absolutely essential for me. To be completely transparent, I discovered it by accident. I don't remember anyone ever teaching it to me. I don't remember reading about it in a book on Bible study or learning it in a class. And yet, I use it every day.

Read out loud.

The beauty of reading out loud is that it isn't an additional step in the Bible study process. It is not something you have to add on. Other than the fact that you probably read a little more slowly when you read out loud, it doesn't take extra time. Since the goal is *liking* the Bible – not just *getting through it* – slowing down a little isn't necessarily a bad thing! In fact, slowing down and reading out loud has some terrific benefits.

YOU WILL FOCUS MORE EASILY.

I have found nothing – other than prayer – that keeps my mind from wandering more effectively than reading out loud. Nothing. When I read silently, it is so easy to let my mind drift from one thought to the next.

How about you? Have you ever gotten a paragraph or two into your Bible reading only to discover you are thinking about something coming up later in your day? Have you ever been reading the Bible, turned the page, and have no idea why? *Well, my eyes were at the bottom. Where was I going to go, the margin?*

Reading out loud hasn't completely solved the problem, but it has helped immensely. Truth be told, there is nothing that will help you focus every time, all the time. That is as ridiculous as the running back who walks over to the coach and says, "Put me in, Coach. I have figured out a way to never get tackled." (Note: If you are a coach, you *can't* put that kid in. He has a concussion.)

Yes, my mind still wanders. In fact, sometimes it wanders two minutes into my reading. But since I started reading out loud, that is really rare. It has become so effective at helping me focus that the only time I *don't* read out loud is if I am in a place where I would be bothering someone. In a coffee shop. On a plane.

I once said that at a workshop only to have someone say, "You should go ahead and read out loud on the plane. Captive audience. Where are they going to go?" Nice. Maybe I will give it a try.

YOU WILL *HEAR* THE BIBLE DIFFERENTLY.

When you read the Bible, does it all sound the same in your head? More specifically, when you read Philippians and you read Galatians, do these two letters sound the same? If so – and please pardon my bluntness – you are reading incorrectly.

Yes, they are both letters. Yes, they are both written by the Apostle Paul. Yes, they are roughly the same length. Yes, they are both printed using the same font in your Bible. But they are massively different in how they *sound*.

Imagine you just received a letter. It is from a dear friend whom you love. You haven't seen this friend in a few years. The very first thing you read (out loud) is:

> *Every time I think of you, I give thanks to my God. Whenever I pray, I make my requests for all of you with joy, for you have been my partners in spreading the Good News about Christ from the time you first heard it until now. And I am certain that God, who began the good work within you, will continue his work until it is finally finished on the day when Christ Jesus returns.*
>
> *So it is right that I should feel as I do about all of you, for you have a special place in my heart. You share with me the special favor of God, both in my imprisonment and in defending and confirming the truth of the Good News. God knows how much I love you and long for you with the tender compassion of Christ Jesus.*
> (Philippians 1:3-8, NLT)

How do you feel? Loved? Cared for? Missed? Hugged?

Now, on a different day you receive another letter from the same friend. Out loud, you read these opening paragraphs:

> *I am shocked that you are turning away so soon from God, who called you to himself through the loving mercy of Christ. You are*

*following a different way that pretends to be
the Good News but is not the Good News at
all. You are being fooled by those who
deliberately twist the truth concerning Christ.*

*Let God's curse fall on anyone, including us or
even an angel from heaven, who preaches a
different kind of Good News than the one we
preached to you. I say again what we have said
before: If anyone preaches any other Good
News than the one you welcomed, let that
person be cursed.* (Galatians 1:6-9, NLT)

How do you feel now? Rebuked? A bit ashamed? Kicked in
the backside?

The Bible is filled with so many different stories,
characters, scenes, and emotions. Reading out loud brings all
those voices to the surface. When I read silently, there is this
little guy who jumps into my brain and reads my Bible for me.
You might not know his name, but I suspect he has shown up
in your brain as well. I call him *Mr. Monotone.*

Has Mr. Monotone ever read your Bible for you? Blah,
blah, blah. How quickly we forget that we are reading the very
words of God Almighty! The Author of Life has written you a
letter. The Inventor of Words has breathed out the Living
Word. And yet, we allow Mr. Monotone to kill it.

YOU WILL REMEMBER MORE.

We remember some of what we see. We remember way more of what we see *and* hear. Even if what we are hearing is our own voice.

In Principle Eight of my book *Like Ice Cream: The Scoop On Helping the Next Generation Fall In Love with God's Word* I wrote about a study that was done in the mid-90's. It was called the Weiss-McGrath report and the focus was on juror retention.

With some jurors, they only presented evidence verbally. Others only saw the evidence. Still others were given the evidence verbally and visually. The results were staggering. They found that after only seventy-two hours, participants retained only 10% of evidence presented verbally. Those who received the information visually retained 20%. Here's the kicker: Those who both heard and saw the evidence retained 65% of the information! It was the *combination* of seeing and hearing that made the difference.

The same is true with the Bible. We will certainly retain some of what we read silently. But if you can more than triple your retention simply by reading out loud, why wouldn't you do it? It is frustrating to put time into reading something and not remembering it. Remembering what we read is a huge part of liking the Bible. And the best way to do that is to read out loud.

Tip 7

Read Alone.

Most of the tips in this book are of the every-time-and-all-the-time variety. Tip 4 (*Watch the whole movie.*) and Tip 5 (*Learn from your shampoo bottle.*) are done specifically when you are beginning a new study of a book or large section of the Bible.

This tip goes right along with those two. It is done at the start of your study. It helps you enjoy it right from the get-go. It sets the stage for enjoying more detailed study later on. And it is something that most people tell me they rarely do (if ever).

Read *only* the Bible. No devotional. No commentary. No questions. No videos. No lesson. Simply you, God, and His Word. That's it.

Before you fire off an email sharing how beneficial your last devotional was, all the ways a specific commentary has helped you, or what you have gleaned from a certain author's insights, hear me out. I love my study tools. The amount of research we have at the click of a mouse is phenomenal. I have no intention of ever giving up my Logos Bible Software™. I read a lot of extra books and commentaries. *Just not at the beginning.*

Probably the best way to make my argument for reading alone is to look at what happens when we *don't* read alone. More specifically, what myths we end up believing when God's Word is always viewed through additional lenses.

MYTH ONE: THE COMMENTARY CARRIES THE SAME WEIGHT AS SCRIPTURE.

Of course, we would never say this out loud. We would never say the commentary is actually God-breathed. But sometimes we unintentionally treat it that way. How can we not? When we read a commentary or devotional every time we read the Bible our brains process them as equals.

Ironically, the most common culprit is a tool that is designed to do exactly the opposite. It is designed to help us know the Word and apply the Word. I have several of them myself. What is the culprit? Your study Bible.

Again, I love my study Bibles. I refer to them quite frequently. However, when I am kicking off a new study, I leave them on the shelf. I purposefully have another Bible that has almost no notes. Otherwise, I will be tempted to read every note. The temptation will win because I am a recovering "ping pong reader."

Are you a ping pong reader? Here is a simple test. When you are reading along in your Bible and come to a bold "a," do you feel an immediate and overwhelming obligation to "ping" down to the bottom of the page, read the note, and then "pong," bounce back up to the top? Then comes that bold "b." Ping...read the note. Pong...back up to the verse. Ping...Pong.

That's me. I am a ping pong reader. It is virtually impossible for me *not* to bounce down to the notes. They are frequently so helpful. They shed so much light and provide clarity. The notes offer application and discussion questions. The maps and diagrams help me visualize what I am reading.

But they are not Scripture.

If we read them just as much as we read the Biblical text – especially in the Ping Pong style – how can we *not* give them the same amount of weight? I am reminded of something I heard a couple decades ago. (Sorry, I can't remember who said it.)

A commentary is nothing more than another Christian's comments on the Bible.

Amen. The notes, books, devotionals, and commentaries are extremely helpful. They offer additional insight, explanation, and perspective we might never come up with on our own.

This is quite similar to the insight a friend might offer. If you are both reading the same book of the Bible, you will each see things the other missed. The conversation will benefit you both. But imagine if every time you got together you said, "I didn't read the Bible at all. What has God told you? What do I need to know? What encouragement do you have for me?"

Seems wrong, doesn't it? You would almost certainly learn some things. You might even enjoy their insights or marvel at how close they are to God. But you would be no closer to liking the Bible yourself, let alone falling in love with the Author!

MYTH TWO: I CAN'T UNDERSTAND THE BIBLE UNLESS SOMEONE EXPLAINS IT TO ME.

So many of us believe this one. Do you? Answer honestly. Do you feel like the Bible is complicated? I spent a long time feeling overwhelmed by the Bible. Don't get me wrong. There is still plenty about the Bible I don't understand. After all, God put a lot in there!

That said, I no longer believe that it is *primarily* difficult. In fact, I believe the opposite. The more I read it, the more I am convinced that a vast majority of what is written in the Bible can be understood by your average eleven-year-old. And yet, the myth lives on.

Let's put your God-given imagination to work. Rewind a few thousand years. You are a fly on the wall in the Throne Room. Father, Son, and Spirit are having a conversation.

> Father: *"We should provide our children with a written relationship guide."*

> Son: *"Fantastic idea! But I think we should make it as confusing as possible."*

> Holy Spirit: *"Couldn't agree more. Oh...and it should probably be boring too."*

What do you think? Absurd, right? This is the same Father who loved you and chose you before the creation of the world (Eph. 1:4). This is the same Son who put on flesh, became the Living Word (John 1:1-18), allowed Himself to be arrested, tortured, and killed, and then conquered death, hell, and the grave so you could hang out with Him forever. This is the same Holy Spirit who guides you (John 16:13) and intercedes with the Father on your behalf (Rom. 8:26-27).

Would this Father, this Son, and this Holy Spirit really try to make understanding His Story something only a few theologians could grasp? A few teachers? A few pastors? While the rest were left to wallow in their confusion? Not a chance.

DEBUNK THE MYTHS.

You are almost done with this chapter. It is time for you to debunk these myths once and for all.

Go pour another cup of coffee. Grab a Bible. (Preferably one with very few notes.) Pick a book. And read. Just you and God. Ask Him to meet you there. Expect Him to meet you there. He will. After all, He has made a habit of doing exactly that for a very long time.

Tip 8

Don't Read Alone.

Do I have you confused? Alone? Not alone? Which is it? Well, both, actually. It all has to do with timing. If we are talking about daily time in God's Word, "alone" is the answer. If we are talking about weekly, bi-weekly, or monthly, the answer expands to "alone *and* not alone."

When it comes to liking the Bible, few habits are more beneficial than having regular conversations with someone – or a small group of people – who is studying the same book of the Bible as you. There are at least four specific ways having a Bible buddy (yeah...cheesy...I know) will help you.

Your buddy will help you be more consistent.

Let's be honest. There is nothing quite like knowing that someone will be checking up on you to improve your consistency. Yes, we should want to read the Bible. Yes, we should pursue our relationship with Christ because that's what we were made for. Yes, time with God in His Word should be at the top of our priority list. These are all true. But take a look at this:

> *Let us hold tightly without wavering to the hope we affirm, for God can be trusted to keep his promise. Let us think of ways to motivate one another to acts of love and good works. And let us not neglect our meeting together, as some people do, but encourage one another, especially now that the day of his return is drawing near.* (Hebrews 10:23-25, NLT)

Did you notice that three different times the author says "Let us." (That phrase shows up a whole bunch of times in

Hebrews by the way.) We were meant to be in this together. We need each other. God knows that we are easily distracted. God knows that there are days when internal motivation is enough, and days when, unfortunately, it is not.

We hate the feeling of committing to something and then having to look that person in the eyes and say, "No. I didn't get the reading done." Oooo...you hate that, don't you? Simply telling someone that you will read – and scheduling a time to discuss it – will make you more consistent. Ideal or not, it just works.

YOUR BUDDY WILL MAKE IT MORE FUN.

Remember being in Boy Scouts or attending summer camp? Wasn't there always a buddy system? The main reason for the buddy system was safety. But it was also more fun. Whether you are canoeing on the lake, hiking the trails, or shooting BB guns – it is way more fun with a buddy.

Having a Bible buddy is more fun. When someone gets excited, you get excited. When someone sees something funny, you are more likely to see it as funny. When someone shares something that challenged them, you will find yourself wondering how you could apply that truth.

There is a concept I have written about in a couple other books that applies here: *Whatever we talk about we get more interested in.*

Think about anything you love. Music. Sports. Movies. Coffee. Ice cream. (These are some of my favorites.) Whatever the topic, how did you first get into it? Chances are pretty high that you knew someone who introduced you to a certain type of music, took you to a ballgame, or taught you how to make "perfect foam" for your cappuccino.

You experienced it with someone.

You talked about it.

You spent time with someone who loved it, and you started to love it. We love to talk, and we talk about what we love. Maybe you couldn't care less about sports. Maybe you like knitting. If so, are there people you could get together with who could talk about yarn, patterns, and past projects all day long?

You *can* get that way with the Bible. You *will* get that way with the Bible. But not if you always – and only – read alone. You need someone to talk with about what you read. You need a buddy.

YOUR BUDDY WILL SEE THINGS YOU MISSED.

You can't catch everything. You won't catch everything. You weren't *meant* to catch everything. We need each other. This is a good thing.

Solomon wasn't kidding when he wrote,

As iron sharpens iron, so a friend sharpens a friend. (Prov. 27:17, NLT)

Left alone, the sharpest knife will grow dull. It needs to be sharpened. So do you. So do I. We need each other if we are going to be as "sharp" as we can possibly be. A knife can't sharpen itself. Neither can you.

It never ceases to amaze me how different people will see so many different details, truths, or applications in the same passage. I can pour over a passage time and again, feeling like I have gleaned everything there is to glean. Inevitably, when I get together with a buddy, he will bring up something that I completely missed.

The same thing happens in our small group each week. We all bring something different to the conversation. As we each share what God revealed to us, we are all encouraged, challenged, and learn. As we do, each of us continually grows in our love for God and His Word.

Whether you meet one-on-one with a buddy, gather with a few other men or women, or get a handful of couples together every other week, you need to read with other people. Until you do, you will only be tasting a small sliver of a really big pie. And come on, who doesn't like more pie?

YOUR BUDDY WILL HELP YOU CLARIFY YOUR OWN THINKING.

Thoughts that stay in your head remain cloudy. As they move through your mind and out your mouth, they will simply sound different. You will realize that what you thought to be true was slightly off. Or the conviction of your mind might become even stronger as you talk about it. Either way, there is great value in talking with another person (or group of people) about what God has been saying to you.

This is very similar to what happens when we journal. I have frequently heard a quote that I completely agree with.

"Thoughts disentangle themselves passing over the lips or through pencil tips."
(Dawson Trotman, founder of The Navigators)

There is something that happens when we talk things out that is freeing and clarifying. It happens when we journal. It happens even more fully when we add discussion to the mix.

Ask a friend if he wants to meet for coffee before work each Tuesday. Find a few friends who will grab lunch together on Thursdays. See if four other couples would set aside every other Sunday evening for dinner and discussion.

Now pick a book of the Bible and have each person read it on their own. When you get together, unpack it. For a couple weeks you might chat about the overarching "big themes" each person noticed. Then start to narrow it down. Discuss a chapter, a story, or even a single verse. Watch what happens.

My prediction? You will find yourself liking the Bible more and looking forward to the next time your group is getting together.

Tip 9

Go On a 60-Day Adventure.

Wwhat would you say if I told you that 60 days from now you could understand and love a book of the Bible more than any you have studied before? Now, what if I told you that you would actually have huge chunks of it down word-for-word without even trying? That would be pretty cool, right?

Well, you can. (Yes, you.)

In my first book – *Falling In Love With God's Word: Discovering What God Always Intended Bible Study To Be* – I lay out my entire approach for how I study the Bible. I am not going to try to explain the whole process in one chapter, but I do want to give you the basics. The 60-Day Adventure is built on the process laid out in that book.

As you have gathered by now, when we approach the Bible the same way our brains naturally and easily learn anything else (from the general to the specific), we enjoy it more and remember it better. In that first book, I put the process into the analogy of building a house. Foundation first. Then Framing. Finally, Finish Work. All are vitally important. So is the *order* in which we do them.

Before laying out the day-by-day plan, here is the ultra-nutshell version of each phase:

FOUNDATION

This is where you get the big picture. This is where *Tip 4*, *Tip 5*, and *Tip 7* come in. Read the whole thing. Read it again. Read alone. This is where you get a feel for the main topics, tone, and thought process of the book.

During the Foundation Phase is also where you do some background studies on the Author, the Audience, and the

Atmosphere. There are lots of tools – online and in print – to help you with this. For more info, you can check out www.keithferrin.com/resources.

FRAMING

The Framing Phase is essentially where you build a bridge between the general study of Foundation and the paragraph-by-paragraph, detailed study found in Finish Work. First, break down the book into major sections. Possibly put it into an outline. I know, the word "outline" might make you cringe with bad memories from high school, but it is very efficient.

Break it down one step further to see where each paragraph or two fits into the broader outline. This isn't the time to *study* each paragraph. You are just putting it into smaller pieces. Think of the first step as the *acts* of a play and the second as jotting down the *scenes* that make up the acts.

FINISH WORK

Once you have laid a Foundation, and done the very quick but very necessary Framing, you are ready for Finish Work. This is when you look for specific life application. Finish Work is the time for meditating on a single paragraph or verse. Study a word or phrase that has shown up several times in that book.

Again, there are lots of resources out there to help you with this. During Finish Work is when I am extremely grateful for my study Bible, numerous Bible websites, and my Logos Bible Software™.

I told you that would be quick. If you want more detailed information, you can visit www.keithferrin.com or order a copy of *Falling In Love With God's Word* from your favorite online retailer.

WHAT BOOK SHOULD I USE FOR THE 60-DAY ADVENTURE?

I almost always recommend starting with either Philippians or II Timothy. The main reason is quite simple: *They are both short.* Anytime you are trying something new, short is good. Philippians takes about 15-20 minutes to read. II Timothy is even shorter. You can easily read either book in a single sitting, whether you have been in the habit of Bible reading or you are just starting out.

There is one more reason I recommend these two books in particular. Each contains a lot of what I refer to as the "Christian Cliché" verses. Not cliché as in lame or silly. Cliché as in verses we hear all the time. Have you ever heard any of these?

> *I thank my God every time I remember you.*
> (Philippians)

> *For God did not give us a spirit of timidity, but a spirit of power, of love and of self-discipline.*
> (II Timothy)

> *For me to live is Christ and to die is gain.*
> (Philippians)

And the things you have heard me say in the presence of many witnesses entrust to reliable men who will also be qualified to teach others. (II Timothy)

And the peace of God, which transcends all understanding, will guard your hearts and your minds in Christ Jesus. (Philippians)

All Scripture is God-breathed... (II Timothy)

Rejoice in the Lord always. I will say it again: Rejoice! (Philippians)

I have fought the good fight, I have finished the race, I have kept the faith. (II Timothy)

I can do everything through Him who gives me strength. (Philippians)

Both books contain a lot more than what's listed here. And yet, if I asked you what Philippians is about, or to summarize II Timothy in a sentence or two, could you do it? When you dive into either of these letters for a couple months it fills in the gaps. It helps you see these familiar verses in a new light. It provides context. People tell me all the time how much more they understand – and enjoy – the books after soaking in the big picture.

A 60-DAY ADVENTURE IN PHILIPPIANS

Foundation

1.   Read Philippians. (Out loud. Remember Tip 4!)
2.   Read Philippians.
3.   Read Philippians.
4.   Read Philippians as if you were Paul sitting in prison.
5.   Read Philippians. Do a Background Study on the Author (Paul). Information can be found in your study Bible, or visit www.keithferrin.com/resources.
6.   Read Philippians in a different translation.
7.   Read Philippians.
8.   Read Philippians as if you were a member of the Philippian church receiving this letter for the first time.
9.   Read Philippians. Do a Background Study on the Audience (Church in Philippi)
10. Read Philippians. Write a one-paragraph summary of Philippians. (Don't overthink this.)
11. Read Philippians. Make a list of the main themes found in Philippians.
12. Read Philippians.
13. Read Philippians. Do a Background Study on the Atmosphere (What was going on at the time? Again, your study Bible will help you or visit www.keithferrin.com/resources.)
14. Read Philippians in a third translation (other than your normal Bible and what you read on Day 6).
15. Read Philippians. Review the summary you wrote on Day 10. See if you can narrow it down to 2-3 sentences.
16. Read Philippians. Form the themes you identified on Day 11 into a *very general* outline.
17. Read Philippians.
18. Read Philippians.
19. Read Philippians.

20. Read Philippians. Pare down what you wrote on Days 10 and 15 into one or two sentences.
21. Read Philippians. Review the outline you wrote on Day 16. Can it be simplified or clarified?
22. Read Philippians in a fourth translation. (Maybe try one of the paraphrases like *The Message* or *The Voice Bible*.)
23. Read Philippians.
24. Read Philippians.
25. Read Philippians. Take what you wrote on Day 20 and get it down to a single, concise sentence.
26. Read Philippians. Finalize the outline you wrote on Day 21.

Framing

27. Read Philippians Chapter 1. Take the outline you finalized on Day 21. Break it down one or two more levels based on each paragraph in Chapter 1.
28. Read Philippians Chapter 2. Take the outline you finalized on Day 21. Break it down one or two more levels based on each paragraph in Chapter 2.
29. Read Philippians Chapter 3. Take the outline you finalized on Day 21. Break it down one or two more levels based on each paragraph in Chapter 3.
30. Read Philippians Chapter 4. Take the outline you finalized on Day 21. Break it down one or two more levels based on each paragraph in Chapter 4.

Finish Work

During the Finish Work Phase, it is time to focus on a few verses, or even a word. You could read it prayerfully, engaging with God about what you read. You might try journaling, writing a song, or drawing a picture. If you teach the Bible, you will find it helpful to add anything you discover through prayer or study to a more-detailed version of your outline.

Word studies can be done online (see www.keithferrin.com/resources), using purchased software, or by obtaining a good Bible dictionary or word study book. Feel free to shoot me a note if you need help getting pointed in the right direction. There is also a whole chapter devoted to this in my first book, *Falling In Love with God's Word*.

In any event, a major focus of Finish Work is not just *understanding* the verses for the day, but also *applying* what God shows you. Life application is how God uses His Word to transform us to be more like Jesus. After all, head knowledge without application will never lead to loving God and His Word!

31. Focus on 1:1-2. Do a word study on "servant."
32. Focus on 1:3-6. Do a word study on "joy."
33. Focus on 1:7-8.
34. Focus on 1:9-11. Do a word study on "pure."
35. Focus on 1:12-14.
36. Focus on 1:15-18a.
37. Do a word study on "selfish ambition."
38. Focus on 1:18b-26.
39. Do a word study on "hope."
40. Read Philippians.
41. Focus on 1:27-30.
42. Focus on 2:1-4.
43. Do a word study on "fellowship."
44. Focus on 2:5-11.
45. Do a word study on "nature." Notice how different Greek words are translated the same in Verses 6 and 7.
46. Focus on 2:12-13.

47. Focus on 2:14-18.
48. Focus on 2:19-24.
49. Focus on 2:25-30. Do a word study on "honor."
50. Read Philippians.
51. Focus on 3:1-6.
52. Focus on 3:7-11.
53. Do a word study on "righteousness."
54. Focus on 3:12-16.
55. Focus on 3:17-4:1.
56. Focus on 4:2-9.
57. Do a word study on "anxious."
58. Focus on 4:10-13. Do a word study on "content."
59. Focus on 4:14-23.
60. Read Philippians.

A 60-Day Adventure in II Timothy

Foundation

1. Read II Timothy. (Out loud. Remember Tip 4!)
2. Read II Timothy.
3. Read II Timothy.
4. Read II Timothy as if you were Paul sitting on Death Row...knowing you won't make it through the winter.
5. Read II Timothy. Do a Background Study on the Author (Paul). Information can be found in your study Bible, or visit www.keithferrin.com/resources.
6. Read II Timothy in a different translation.
7. Read II Timothy.
8. Read II Timothy as if you were Timothy. Your good friend and mentor is writing from Death Row with some final words and a desperate plea to come visit him soon.
9. Read II Timothy. Do a Background Study on the Audience (Timothy)
10. Read II Timothy. Write a one-paragraph summary of II Timothy. (Don't overthink this.)
11. Read II Timothy. Make a list of the main themes found in II Timothy.
12. Read II Timothy.
13. Read II Timothy. Do a Background Study on the Atmosphere (What was going on at the time? Again, your study Bible will help you or visit www.keithferrin.com/resources.)
14. Read II Timothy in a third translation (other than your normal Bible and what you read on Day 6).
15. Read II Timothy. Review the summary you wrote on Day 10. See if you can narrow it down to 2-3 sentences.
16. Read II Timothy. Form the themes you identified on Day 11 into a *very general* outline.
17. Read II Timothy.

18. Read II Timothy.
19. Read II Timothy.
20. Read II Timothy. Pare down what you wrote on Days 10 and 15 into one or two sentences.
21. Read II Timothy. Review the outline you wrote on Day 16. Can it be simplified or clarified?
22. Read II Timothy in a fourth translation. (Maybe try one of the paraphrases like *The Message* or *The Voice Bible*.)
23. Read II Timothy.
24. Read II Timothy.
25. Read II Timothy. Take what you wrote on Day 20 and get it down to a single, concise sentence.
26. Read II Timothy. Finalize the outline you wrote on Day 21.

Framing

27. Read II Timothy Chapter 1. Take the outline you finalized on Day 21. Break it down one or two more levels based on each paragraph in Chapter 1.
28. Read II Timothy Chapter 2. Take the outline you finalized on Day 21. Break it down one or two more levels based on each paragraph in Chapter 2.
29. Read II Timothy Chapter 3. Take the outline you finalized on Day 21. Break it down one or two more levels based on each paragraph in Chapter 3.
30. Read II Timothy Chapter 4. Take the outline you finalized on Day 21. Break it down one or two more levels based on each paragraph in Chapter 4.

Finish Work

During the Finish Work Phase, it is time to focus on a few verses, or even a word. You could read it prayerfully, engaging with God about what you read. You might try journaling, writing a song, or drawing a picture. If you teach the Bible, you will find it helpful to add anything you discover through prayer or study to a more-detailed version of your outline.

Word studies can be done online (see www.keithferrin.com/resources), using purchased software, or by obtaining a good Bible dictionary or word study book. Feel free to shoot me a note if you need help getting pointed in the right direction. There is also a whole chapter devoted to this in my first book, *Falling In Love with God's Word*.

In any event, a major focus of Finish Work is not just *understanding* the verses for the day, but also *applying* what God shows you. Life application is how God uses His Word to transform us to be more like Jesus. After all, head knowledge without application will never lead to loving God and His Word!

31.   Focus on 1:1-5.
32.   Do a word study on "apostle."
33.   Focus on 1:6-7.
34.   Focus on 1:8-12.
35.   Focus on 1:13-14.
36.   Do a word study on "guard."
37.   Focus on 1:15-18.
38.   Focus on 2:1-7.
39.   Focus on 2:8-13. Do a word study on "endure."
40.   Read II Timothy.
41.   Focus on 2:14-19.
42.   Do a word study on "correctly handles."
43.   Focus on 2:20-21.
44.   Do a word study on "made holy."
45.   Focus on 2:22-26.
46.   Focus on 3:1-5.

47. Do a word study (or several!) on any of the words in 3:1-5.
48. Focus on 3:6-9.
49. Focus on 3:10-13.
50. Read II Timothy.
51. Focus on 3:14-17.
52. Do a word study on "God-breathed/inspired."
53. Focus on 4:1-2.
54. Focus on 4:3-5.
55. Focus on 4:6-8.
56. Focus on 4:9-13.
57. Focus on 4:14-15.
58. Focus on 4:16-18.
59. Focus on 4:19-22.
60. Read II Timothy.

Tip 10

Take Two 4-Month Challenges.

 By now, you have probably noticed that I am a pretty big fan of getting the "big picture." These two challenges will help you get the big picture. Two big pictures actually. Let's look at the first...

Challenge One: The Bible Read Thru

Until a few years ago, I didn't realize how helpful - and enjoyable - it would be to get the really, *really* big picture. Not until a woman who had taken my Falling *in Love with God's Word Workshop* sent me an email with a link to an article by Ron Frost.

Ron is a pastoral consultant for Barnabas International (www.barnabas.org) and was a professor at Multnomah University (www.multnomah.edu) for twenty years. The article tells of when he was a young man, and of a retired missionary who inspired him to simply read the Bible - two to three times every year! Ron took the challenge and has been doing exactly that for the last several decades. I was intrigued to say the least.

Soon after reading the article, I reached out to Ron, and he agreed to have lunch with me. We sat at a small, waterfront restaurant in Seattle and chatted about our mutual love for the Living Word. I walked away *knowing* that I needed to do what Ron calls a "Bible Read Thru."

I knew I had to do it. I knew it would be valuable. I just didn't want to. It seemed like too much time. I ignored the Voice for a couple months. Then came New Year's, and along with it...resolutions. "Okay, God. I'll do it."

Heeding Ron's advice, I didn't try it alone. (Remember *Tip 8?*) I invited the men at my church's January men's breakfast to join me. Five other guys took the challenge. To a person, all six of us found it extremely enjoyable and valuable.

We were also blown away at how much *easier* it was than any of us expected. In fact, one of the guys finished in seventy-three days! *And he had never read the Bible before.* In fact, he didn't even own a Bible. The week before we started, he had to grab one of the paperback Bibles we hand out at church.

That first Bible Read Thru was started in January 2010. I have now done it every year since (and have no plans to stop anytime soon). It is my January-through-April ritual.

There are only three simple parameters:

One: Read the whole Bible in four months.

You can read Genesis to Revelation straight through. You can read using a chronological Bible. (There is a blog post with several different chronological outlines on www.keithferrin.com. Search on "chronological.") You can read an Old Testament book, New Testament, then back to the Old Testament. However you want. Just read it. The whole thing.

If you are thinking this is an oh-my-goodness-I-could-never-do-that commitment, allow me to put it in perspective. The average audio Bible is a little over seventy hours. That even includes the sound effects for animals, musicians, and storms. Multiply by sixty minutes and divide that by 122 (the number of days in a four-month stretch) and your daily commitment is about thirty-five minutes. Is it a step up from what you are doing now? Possibly. Is it an insurmountable challenge? Hardly.

I highly encourage you to simply set aside forty-five to sixty minutes a day. That way, even allowing for the pauses to underline or jot down a quick note, you will always be ahead. There will be days when you can only squeeze in ten minutes because you are swamped with work, school, or your kid's baseball tournament. There will be days when you've got the flu and can't read at all. If you build in a habit of reading a little extra, those days won't set you back.

Whatever you do, *don't* break it down into how much you have to "get through" each day. Your mindset will be all wrong. It will very quickly become a chore. And when you miss a day, you will spend days or weeks playing catch up. No fun. Even if you have broken it down so you can read chronologically, use the breakdown as a guide for what passages you need to be reading, not the specific amount per day you have to get through.

Two: Read with a pen in your hand.

If you are an "underliner," underline. If not, take notes in a journal. You can also use a virtual notepad like OneNote or Evernote. Find some way to keep track of the conversations you have with God as you read.

Whatever method you choose, it is important to remember that you are not outlining or writing down details. This is a Bible *Read Thru.* It is not a Bible *study.* Simply jot down anything that stands out, challenges you, or even confuses you. Stay in the big story. Who knows? The notes you jot down during this four-month stretch might just be the guide for the deeper study you do the rest of the year!

Three: Talk about it.

If you want to get the most out of your Bible Read Thru, this third parameter is not optional. You will be tempted to make it optional. It will seem easier to keep it between you and God. You will convince yourself that you don't need the accountability to stick with it.

First off, accountability is a good thing, and you probably do need it. That said, accountability isn't the main reason the third parameter is in here. Remember: This book is about *liking* the Bible. Talking about it will help you like it. That's why I devoted a whole chapter in this book to having a Bible buddy.

Most of the time, I have gotten together with a group of three to six men. Last year, there were a couple women who joined us. There was certainly value found in each scenario. I have no hard-and-fast guidance here.

However, I do recommend having a minimum of three people (and preferably four to six). That way, when someone is traveling, sick, or accidentally oversleeps, you don't end up skipping a week.

I have heard of people doing this part with their weekly small group, after school, or even with some coworkers over the lunch break. The Bible Read Thru groups I have assembled have always met at a coffee shop (my home away from home) early in the morning on a weekday.

When you get together, keep it very simple. First off, decide how much time you are going to spend just chatting. If you set aside ten minutes to catch up on family, work, or the weekend's ballgame, then you will stick to it. If you don't set a time, you will get thirty minutes in and someone will say, "Oh, look at the time. I guess we better hustle through this." Not the approach you are looking for.

Have each person share one of the things they wrote down or underlined. Read the passage if it's not too long. Focus on the Word, and the conversations you each had with God throughout the week. Resist the urge to answer every question, or turn it into a discussion about what a passage means, or what each of you thinks about what someone else shared. Keep in mind that you will have each read about 50-80 chapters of the Bible since you last met! If you have an in-depth conversation about every verse someone underlined, you will need to meet *daily,* not weekly!

Read it in four months. Read with a pen in your hand. Talk about it. That's it. Take the challenge. Four months from now, your love for the Word, understanding of the Word, and appreciation of the Word will all be greatly increased.

CHALLENGE TWO: THE NEW DISCIPLE CHALLENGE

I call this one the "New Disciple Challenge" not because it is only for new Christ-followers, but because it is definitely where I recommend a new disciple should *start*. If you have only recently begun hanging out with Jesus, then you need to, well, hang out with Jesus.

Note: If you have been walking with Christ a long time, you might want to begin with a Bible Read Thru or one of the 60-Day Adventures from the last chapter. That said, I highly recommend taking this second challenge every so often just to keep your heart and mind focused on the person, work, teaching, and mission of Jesus.

The parameters for the New Disciple Challenge are even simpler than the last one:

One: Focus on only five books.

During these four months you will only read Matthew, Mark, Luke, John, and Acts. Here is a quick overview of each:

Matthew – Matthew (also known as Levi) was a tax collector who became one of Jesus' twelve disciples and traveled with Jesus during the approximately three years of His earthly ministry. He focuses pretty heavily on Jesus as the Messiah/King and how Jesus fulfills Old Testament prophecies (facts and predictions about future events).

Mark – Mark (also known as John Mark) was not one of the twelve disciples. He traveled with the Apostle Paul on his first missionary journey. He focuses on Jesus' humble servant attitude. What He did, what He taught, and how He lived.

Luke – Luke was a doctor, as well as a close friend and traveling companion of the Apostle Paul. He is the only known Gentile (non-Jewish) author in the New Testament. Luke is the "detail guy." He paints a clear picture of Jesus as the perfect Son of Man.

John – John was one of the twelve disciples (so was his older brother James) and refers to himself as "the disciple Jesus loved." He is out to show his readers that Jesus is not only fully human, but He is fully God as well. As we come to know Jesus' humanity and divinity, we also see that real, abundant, eternal life can only come through Him.

Acts – Luke is also the author of Acts. In the book of Acts, Luke gives an account of the formation, growth, success, and struggles of the early church. The first third of the book focuses primarily on the work and teaching of Peter (one of the twelve disciples). The latter two-thirds focus on the conversion of the Apostle Paul (previously a Christian hater and killer) and his three missionary journeys.

Two: Read each book for two weeks.

There isn't a set number of times you need to read each book. Determine how much time you will set aside each day for reading. Obviously, if you read for forty-five minutes each day you will read each book more times than if you read only for twenty. That said, even reading twenty minutes each day will have you walking through each book at least twice in a two-week period.

Some of you might be concerned about my math skills. Yes, this is a four-month challenge. Yes, you will only read five books. Yes, you will read each for two weeks. However, you will read Acts *after each gospel.* Here's how it goes: Read Matthew for two weeks. Then read Acts for two weeks. Then Mark for two weeks. *Back to Acts for two weeks.* Then Luke. Then Acts. Then John. Finish with two weeks in Acts.

By the end of the four months, you will have read four different accounts of the life of Jesus and the history of the early church several times. This overview will provide an extremely solid foundation, whether your next study takes you back into the Old Testament or into a 60-Day Adventure into one of the letters of the New Testament.

Three: Talk about it.

Yes, the Buddy Rule still applies. You will get way more out of it if you are reading with someone. It is vital – especially for new disciples – to develop a habit of meeting with others to discuss, question, wrestle with, and process God's Word.

If you skipped the last section about the Bible Read Thru – and you want to find out more about the benefits of this third parameter – hop back about a thousand words. It's all there waiting for you.

Let's Connect...

So, what do you think? I am genuinely interested.

There are some things I know, and lots more that I don't. I need your voice. I need to hear your ideas, thoughts, struggles, and hopes.

- *What are you still struggling with?*
- *What tips would you add?*
- *How can I serve you?*
- *How can I serve your church, small group, or university?*
- *What would you like to see me write about on my blog? In my next book?*
- *What resource would you like me to create?*

There are lots of ways we can connect. Here are a couple:

- Email: keith@keithferrin.com
- Blog: www.keithferrin.com

I'm also pretty easy to find on Facebook, Twitter, Pinterest, and Google+. Just search for "keithferrin."

If you would like to see some clips of what I do or find out more about bringing me to your conference, university, church, or event, the best place to start is www.keithferrin.com/speaking.

Thanks for reading. Writing without reading is, well, no fun. I truly appreciate you spending your time with me.

My prayer is that the next time you pick up your Bible, you will like it just a little more than last time. And then a little more the next time...and a little more...and...

Ok...I think I'm done. Go read your Bible. It's outstanding. Really.

Alongside,
Keith

About the Author

Keith Ferrin is a speaker, storyteller, and author who strives to help people realize that the living Word of God is a reality – not a phrase. He actually holds to the idea that people can believe the Bible is not only true and applicable, but also fun, engaging, and enjoyable. (Hence the reason for this book.)

He founded That You May Know Ministries in 1996 to help people fall in love with God's Word and its Author. His one-man, dramatic, word-for-word presentations of whole books of the Bible have been seen by audiences of hundreds and thousands, by young kids, college students, and old (ahem) "seasoned" folks.

He is a husband to one, and a father to three. And he thinks the world is a better place since the invention of coffee and ice cream (not necessarily in that order).

Take "10 Tips" to the Next Level...

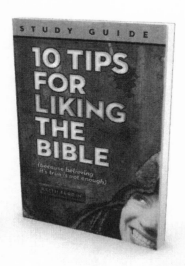

PERFECT FOR SMALL GROUPS, YOUTH GROUPS, AND SUNDAY SCHOOL CLASSES!

- Additional thoughts for every tip written by Keith Ferrin.
- Questions for discussion and application.
- Space for your additional thoughts, notes, and questions.
- Additional Scripture references for going deeper – on your own or with your group.

You can purchase the Study Guide on Amazon, or download the PDF for free at www.keithferrin.com/10tipsbonuses!

Use password: likethebible

Get Keith's entire process...

Falling in Love with God's Word
(Discovering What God Always Intended Bible Study to Be)

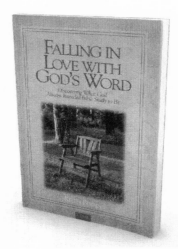

- Unpacks every aspect of Foundation, Framing, and Finish Work.
- Go in depth on everything from Foundational Reading, to discovering a book's theme and purpose, to diving into detailed word studies.

"Falling in Love with God's Word made the Bible come alive. His insight into the studying of Scripture shows not only the importance of knowing God's Word, but also gives all who use his material a deeper love for Jesus."

Twiggs Reed
National Director for Young Life (Singapore)

Are you a parent, youth pastor, or children's pastor? If so...this is for you!

Like Ice Cream

(The Scoop on Helping the Next Generation Fall in Love with God's Word)

I am a parent of three young children. I was a youth pastor for six years. I have an M.Ed. in Guidance and Counseling and spent a couple years as an elementary school counselor. (Oh, and my wife has taught elementary school for seventeen years.) **We love the next generation.** And we want our kids – and yours – to grow up loving the Bible, not just believing it's true.

"Like Ice Cream is a marvelous book. If we can pass on a love for God's Word to our children, we are giving them a gift that will last a lifetime. Keith offers the most practical, effective approach I have ever seen to accomplish just that."

Gary Thomas
Writer in Residence, 2nd Baptist Church, Houston, TX
Author of *Sacred Marriage* and *Sacred Parenting*

Made in the USA
Charleston, SC
09 October 2014